Bottom Dog Press

Huron, Ohio

Baltic Amber in a Chest

Clarissa Jakobsons

Harmony Writing Series
Bottom Dog Press
Huron, Ohio

ISBN: 978-1-947504-37-0
Bottom Dog Press, Inc.
PO Box 425, Huron, OH 44839
Lsmithdog@aol.com
http://smithdocs.net

CREDITS:

General Editor: Larry Smith
Cover & Layout Design: Susanna Sharp-Schwacke
Cover Art: Clarissa Jakobsons, *My Head*, Oil on Canvas

DEDICATION:

To my husband, Andris for his encouragement; my daughters, Lara and Marielle; as well as to my dear grandchildren, Lucas and Mila.

Contents

peace

an orchid emerges

dry leaves

i sit on stones

The disadvantage of men not knowing the past
is that they do not know the present.

—G.K. Chesterton

I carry these poems and memories
in heavy pockets and dreams built
on blood filled foundations
of bones, myth, and meditations.
I carry these poems and memories
in heavy pockets and dreams built
on blood filled foundations
of bones, myth, and meditations.

—Clarissa Jakobsons

PROLOGUE FOR *BALTIC AMBER IN A CHEST*

The disruptive effects of war on a family's life often last a lifetime, particularly if the family becomes a displaced casualty of that war. This was the case for the poet's family who fled Lithuania before the Soviet invasion in June of 1940. Both parents were forced to live under a repressive Nazi regime in Germany during the second World War: mother sent to a German slave labor munitions camp in Duderstadt in 1941; father to St. Andreasberg, a German silver-mining town. He fled to Poland, where he was captured and sent to a series of concentration camps for six and a half years, then at the end of the war to the Stalingrad gulag.

The poet was born a year before the war ended and lived with her mother in a small apartment in Hildesheim, Germany, wanting for the basic necessities. In 1949, mother and child emigrated to Chicago. Clarissa didn't meet her father until she was 12, when her mother was able to save enough money from her job at Joe's Dry Goods Store to pay for his Atlantic crossing.

These events paint the backdrop of a lyric account of a life shaped by the hardships of the war and its aftermath. Such an aftermath influences how a person builds a normal and purposeful life while coming to terms with a legacy of sorrow stemming from a world war, as well as from within one's own wounded family.

In *The Tempest*, Antonio states, "What's past is prologue." Indeed, the war supplies the context for this collection of poems constructed from memories both clear and dream-like, artifacts and documents discovered in a trunk, historical research, and a Baltic heritage that strongly informs the poet's sense of identity.

Through this collection, the poet bears witness to the suffering caused by WWII—suffering that reaches beyond a single family to the ripple effect of persecution caused by all wars. She asks the reader to pay attention, to not look away, to be mindful of how evil works in the world, because by doing so, we may not repeat it.

—Barbara Sabol, author of *Imagine a Town*
November 2022

shredded birch leaves
fill a jigsaw puzzle

Father's Parker Pen

I clutch his hand
written answers
for reparations
to the German
government written
seventy years ago—
your Parker pen
rests in a hidden cobweb,
sweaty fingers cannot
release this worn
document—
I read his answers
to blunt questions
one-hundred times
Papers dissolve
sandwiched between
archival love—Father,
today I found the wooden
spoon you hand carved
in a concentration camp
so you could eat

Visiting My Birthplace, Hildesheim 2004

I was baptized at St. Elizabeth's *Kirche,* church,
the only city church not bombed in 1945.
Yesterday's bricks mingle with today's asphalt
against flickering sunspots on medieval domes.

Crossing *Goethe Strasse*, street, two girls pass
the soccer field, their black T-shirts wave against white
letters, *Who was your Mummy?* Previously, I opened
Mother's letter—*Don't forget, you ran away from home.*
It was a terrible thing. But, I was 21, now I'm 61.

At times a forgotten loneliness nags in her letters.
My husband left me alone to struggle. He was a good man.
Yes, Father saved lives during WWII, but he was
incarcerated while Mother struggled searching
for my baby milk the landlady stole.

Dry years struggle to bloom while we scrambled
to survive and breathe. Who was my mother?
Who is she now? We parted. She willed one dollar
to a forgotten daughter not to contest. *Thy will be done.*

Chattering women cross the street corner, hurried
steps hold cellophane wrapped pastries and dangling
cadmium yellow ribbons. Pink peonies bloom
near sidewalks, faded rhododendrons, fuchsia,
and titanium white orchids line *Schiller Strasse*

windowsills. A sign advertises Nadja Naderie's
Wellness Theater, adjacent to transparent yellow
trash bags across the street. A man opens his red
Mercedes for a smiling princess, her wind-tangled
hair glistens in the speeding convertible.

At the next corner, I wiggle the weathered
iron latch of a cemetery gate, years erased
gothic letters. Above a second story-window
a dove perches, spreading her wings.

Ragged Trail of Bones

After historical research by Daniel W. Michaels, retired
Defense Department Analyst and Fulbright scholar

In articles and firsthand texts I learned that under the Yalta
provisions, the U.S., UK., and Russia agreed to use German POWs
in gulag reparations. Each laborer received a bit of black rye.
Productive workers earned a bit of meat, sugar, vegetables, or rice.
The last man called to work-detail is always shot.
Almost a million POWs died after a decade of forced labor,
only 10,000 men survived. My father lived.

In 1945, Brit and U.S. authorities ordered German militia forces
to deport thousands of Lithuanians, Latvians, and Estonians to
Soviet camps. Cattle-cars transported nine-million prisoners,
including my father. Selected women were raped, paraded naked
in front of camp officials with promises of easier workloads for sex.

One out of three inmates died the first year. By 1953, 12–20 million
perished succumbing to exposure, hunger, exhaustion, and malnutrition.
A wooden marker with the deceased inmate's identity was affixed to
the left leg. Gold fillings were extracted by prying or cutting;
skulls hammer-smashed, chests spiked with metal rods.
Bodies thrown into unmarked graves.

Somehow Father survived Nazi concentration camps and the Stalingrad
gulag. Released without any reason. He never mentioned the ordeals
his bones harbored. Without question, silence reigned in our home.
He spent days in quiet labor at the Solon Medical office, Bedford,
and VA hospitals; doctoring patients to live. I search while the gulag
system disappears from our landscape. What can I say or do but
remember to cleanse the empty shoes lining riverbeds.

The Wind Roots an Oak

My birth exploded with B-17s and idle fountain pen markings on yellow-stained roots. Today's faded, torn, and tattered documents reveal World War II death camps. Silence ruled our household, over fifty million families disintegrated during the war: phalanges buried in Germany, femurs in Poland, metatarsals in Siberia, a shattered torso solidified in Lithuania, four-chamber hearts resuscitated in France. Amber nuggets in a chest was found on Erie shores.

Indigo Skies

A poem accepts silence, small prayer
          seeds sprout from gray despair,
deeper than thick moss spreading
          over lawns and ancient bricks.
Gifts nourish. We share our landscape—

black-eyed Susans, monarchs, and milkweed
          washing words off streaked mirrors.
Breath inhales patience,
          let the prayer flags fray,
and burn their sacredness on the wind.

Ink and Dreams

Seize words deep in the incense of light.
Fire-gold lanterns never fail.

Ripped, torn, and shredded dreams
wake tears meshing our eyelids and lashes

joining the past to present tense.
At times, love puzzles into insanity.

We love our tribe, yet a sister, brother,
or parent may erase our writings

and images of a past life. Banished.
Writing a life is no easy task, at times

the ink is invisible, covered in dust.
But we untie the ribbons, open boxes.

Sifting Precious Nuggets

Explore the ancient Baltic
          shores, curl toes
into white sand, sifting
          precious nuggets
through your fingertips
          like a child kissing stones.

Grab an amber nugget
          hold it tight—
claim life before the birds of dawn
          wake for the soul
          of a cheetah that purrs.

Darkness Surrounds

Flashing lights break the stillness.
Impatiently I wait for azaleas, peonies,
        lilacs,
        apple blossoms,
        hydrangeas,
        and Bing cherries
        to bloom
        fragrant springs.

Adam's Rose

It is a vapour that appeareth for a little time, and then vanisheth.
—James 4:14

Verdant blades carpet
Adam's walk. It is good.
Cobalt waters gather in the Baltic
Sea under Vacarinė, Evening Star,
he quivers, whispering Rose's name.

Did they know
that the whispers would lead to falling holly
oak, ash seeds, and the demise of an age
birthing swords between you and me?

Ars Moriendi

Fragmented—

November leaves
circle earth
like memories.
A glimmer
of sun settles
beyond open doors.
Giltinė, the Lithuanian
death mistress,
stings; her lanky
tongue chokes breath.
Bones pulverize
while Vėlė, the ghost,
spins silk shadows
in the fog. Beyond
the open window
Terra prepares an altar
with tears that never dry.

The Last Stronghold

Breslau, the last stronghold of the Third Reich
against Soviet forces was scene to a siege lasting
14 weeks that cost the lives of 170,000 civilians.
An estimated 70% of the city was destroyed
by the Red Army.

Friends, I have secrets to share about forced labor. I found
yellow stained letters, tied and bundled, buried years under
fountain pen papers…Sunlight brightens these rippled brown
fractured cobwebs in my sweaty hands. Father's ebony ink
flowed from a nib pen as I scribble in this journal.

Consular Branch Office of the Political Adviser, Frankfurt am Main, May 1950

Personalfragenboden

Birthplace: Pomedziai, Lithuania
Eye Color: Blue
Profession: Physician
Internment: Thorn, Breslau, Posen, Leslau, and Stalingrad: 6 years, 4 months, 12 days Lager camps: #5771 and #2102

Father, which was worse, Stalin's Gulag or Hitler's
Concentration Camps? Did holy shoe-soles burn
snow-blood rivers, warming log-stacked bodies?
Spirits prowl on flimsy records.

Why Did You Leave Your Homeland: Fear of Russian Communists.
Lineage: Father died when I was six. Mother disappeared in 1943.
Languages: I can speak and write Lithuanian, German, English, Russian, and Polish.

And I remember parental tongues rolling Lithuanian-Polish-Russian words into one scrambled secret sentence.

English Name: Mickevicius Polish Name: Mitskewitsch
Destination: I want to be reunited with my family in Chicago.

The years have blown your ashes
into the 700-year-old Lithuanian family tombstone.
Bare trees remain. The only witnesses.

teardrops
etch windowpanes
you disappear

I Am

named after *Schwester*, Sister, Klarissa—
clear, bright, illustrious. Her arms cradled
my fresh breath for two weeks

toward the end of WWII, in Hildesheim,
near Hannover, Germany. After 60 years we meet—
he called me daughter, *tochter*. From the corner chair

dim lights magnified her brilliant smile.
We spoke a language torn between continents,
gluing war-stained puzzles. There's always a war

to discuss: a city, a name, as remorse turns
to gratitude. The Thousand Year Hildesheim
Rose still blooms with Schwester.

NOCTURNE

At 2 a.m. 250 British-American bomber aircraft started the attack. In 15 minutes, they dropped 438.8 tons of high explosives and 624 tons of incendiary bombs Almost 74% of the Hildesheim buildings were destroyed or damaged including nearly the entire historical city center

—Bomber Command Summary of Operations,
Serial No. 1042, Air Historical Branch, London,
March 1945.

Beyond medieval towers, Schwester Klarissa spoke
of Hildesheim's street patterns when fire trucks

dashed at dawn as British bombers slivered light
beyond earth's shelter. Twenty-year-old Schwester

stumbled down St. Bernward *Krankenhaus*, hospital,
stairs carrying each patient from their fifth-floor

bed to the basement shelter. Repeating this task
when American bombs plagued indigo skies.

Her head leaned back, ankles crossed
for a momentary sigh. Schwester counted the sick

until sirens blasted the cosmos. Repeating
these steps twice daily until all were safe

from combat planes piercing darkness. Air raids
streaked across titanium skies. Schwester hid

two Jewish female doctors from the Nazis.
I received a letter from one of the sisters.

Behind Two-Year-Old Eyes

Oil painting by Rostalski, 1946

Pale veneer
                        masks fear
despairing   hollowed
                        face
always hungry
            her
wisdom   earned
                        too early
dreading
            blasting
bombs   she still
            searches

Displaced Forever

A child skims Borden's Dairy milk
she did not have in Germany
during the war.

Walking to school
she holds a kerchief to her nose
against the stockyard stench.

She loses her way
dodging Chicago streetcars,
lost on the streets of her new home.

Emerald Street Shadows

A coal furnace warmed our living room. On Tuesdays and Fridays,
the iceman claw-hooked glaciers to his back. From the window,

I watched his frame buckle against the truck, bracing frozen blocks
with picks and tongs, then I raced to gather ice chips off asphalt

for summer's delight. Aunt Mary and Cousin Bill shared a bed;
Aunt Betty slept in her own room. Mother and I shared the third bed.

There were no drawers for preciousness, just one steamer trunk.
Nightly window shadows beamed against Hebrew National sausages

hung on ropes. Hungry imagined bites, sausages and me sucking
my thumb under sheets. One window, one closet, one bed.

My First English Lesson

I was four, speaking only German
at St. George's School. Two grades
shared one room, one nun. She
scowled down the aisles,

her black robe slapped our legs.
A wooden ruler hammered tiny fingers
on desks as she demanded the golden rule:
Hold your pencil properly.

Once, kneeling during morning mass,
urine trickled down my legs into a puddle.
Hail Mary's rambled under my breath.
Save me, Jesus.

The nun pasted a black star
on my forehead, it never fell off.

A Child's Christmas Dream, 1954

Marshall Field & Co., State Street, Chicago

Curl
inside the *Pink Marble Ice Cream Parlor*
for a hot fudge sundae

Visit
the Budget Floor Dinette
for the absolute thickest,
heaviest, creamiest
scrambled eggs

Gulp
a snowman sundae
with a bag of day-old
chocolate chips

Line-up
at Santa's Cozy Cottage
with your very own wish list

Save
each penny for next year's treat.

MARSHALL FIELD & COMPANY, CODE OF ETHICS

To do the right thing, at the right time, in the right way;
to do some things better than they were done before;
to eliminate errors; to know both sides of the question;
to be courteous; to be an example; to love our work;
to anticipate requirements; to develop resources;
to recognize no impediments; to master circumstances;
to act from reason rather than rule;
to be satisfied with nothing short of perfection.

The Ultimate Amber Test

I rummage drawers for fossilized amber; pinesap aged millions
of years in a colorful range: honey dew, milk white, cognac,
green,black, or rare violet. Once prescribed for: arthritis,
headaches, heartaches, stomach, spleen, kidney, aching
joints, or teething babies. A travelers' talisman and
early Christian symbol of courage. Egyptians
placed amber in a beloved casket to ensure
the body remained whole. Amber instills
a carefree, sunny disposition dissolving
opposition. Grab a nugget, $2.99
online, shipping extra.

When I was a Chicago brat,
Mother dragged me to Marshall Field
& Co. on State Street to replace a piece
of broken amber on her Lithuanian bracelet.
Weeks later we returned to pick it up. Mother removed
a small piece of 100% wool from her purse and a tiny square
of tissue paper for the ultimate test. She rubbed the new amber
on pure wool placing a tiny square of tissue paper on top. It
did not rise. Her thunder voice shook Tiffany's dome, *This
is not amber, replace this with real amber.* Again, we traveled
on two buses to Marshall Field's for the final amber
test, this stone was half the original size. Mother's
tissue paper rose like a flag at a 90-degree angle,
creating a static charge. Lesson learned.

Your Voice

Expectations sting mother.

Remember this photo of Sandra
Nadel and me at Mr. Comikoff's
Russian Ballet School, in Chicago?

Sandra's arabesque leg soared above mirrors
almost touching the ceiling, black tights
warmed her modest body while

my white cotton panties flaunted
under Aphrodite's transparent aqua,
off-shoulder tunic.

Mother yelled, *Lift your leg*
higher, higher. Higher up!
Finally, I cried, *I can't.*

My limb spasms fell short of the Milky Way.
Photos never lie.

Disoriented and Lost

Mr. Comicoff ordered steel insert
    pointe-shoes for all. Mine were sweat-
stained, crimson leather with grosgrain ribbons.
    Two evening classes per week
and a few private sessions—afterwards
    he opened the door to his bedroom
    and stroked my private parts.

These eight-year-old bones walked and stood
    lonely under Minsky's Burlesque Theater
billboards on State Street—fearful to gaze
    into the stark lights and bleak skies
waiting for two buses homeward.
    Lost under stars.

The Bittersweet Vowel of the Wind

Adieu,
the sword of a dream
thrusts into reality:
Mother Rose once said,
You are ugly,
I don't know you.

I held my firstborn
tight against my breast
as Mother gnawed
our fragile connection.
A jagged sinkhole
swells inside this chest.

Her amber
suitcase overflows
with heirlooms
marked, dated,
but clearly meant
for someone else.

Illinois Home of Mercy

Cremate
that winding nonstop telephone message
at 10:30 pm on the answer machine—
the voice repeats over and over:
Your Mother is dead.

That voice continues:
The body must be removed
within two hours.
But, I live in Ohio.
Did she die alone?
Hospice promised
she would not die alone.

November leaves quiver on the sidewalk.
How much does forgiveness cost?
Fingers polish amber beads.

Earth Mother, Žemyna

Our goddess, you have given me life, you feed me, and carry me.
After death I will rest in you
—Ancient Lithuanian prayer

The ice on Lake Superior has melted.
For the first time my footprints hesitate
following forgotten words on McClean Street.
Spiders weave their wavering canvas under dim lights.
Walking down Aunt Betty's basement stairs
I choose items: Father's Royal Champion typewriter,
Dictaphone, his carved wooden spoon, leather bundled
sepia photographs, and Mother's maroon leather
purse that sailed across the Atlantic. A lost era, european
destinations sailed on Hitler postage stamps
to my home with forgotten smoky and crimson
oil paintings. I found Mother's secret hand-
scrawled diagnosis—*character disorder, superiority complex,*
someone in the family killed another.

Mother spat on nurses, never mentioned
dialysis. Strange how the present heals
the past or the past heals itself, I have been told.
Speak to the earth and it will speak to you.
Come back and visit, Mother once said. I kiss
the past tense, notes scooped into paper
bags, and mirrors that held our tongues.
Let's trade my yellow carnations for a smile,
let our words dance through the night.
There's a Lithuanian belief that the dying
should be laid on earth to lessen suffering.
Even now loved ones scatter a handful
of soil on the dead so that Žemyna treads light,
touches us with loving arms and a heavy breast.

Threshold Conversation

Drab dressed winter, a steady snow,
a frosty mist against treetop faces.

I press Cousin Bill's doorbell three times,
his mud-smeared shoes prop the wooden door.

Bill's hair dangles like Medusa's twin, trailing tentacles
rest on his burnt sienna jacket like a strange

woodsman from another country. We shared
past apartments on Emerald and Lowe Streets,

in Bridgeport, Chicago's DP, Displaced Persons,
playground. He played priest, I a novice

draped in cotton sheets genuflecting at your feet.
Candle offerings echoed Latin refrains

until flames extinguished prayers, scorching
our cardboard sacristy. Remember your hand

stroking my panties. Today your palsied fingers
hold Mother's boxed ashes. Your other palm

offers her gold chain bracelet. Too short,
too tight it strangles my wrist.

Mother's Photo

Rose petals shimmer *mamytė's* portrait
framing her porcelain face, hidden
under a straw hat blowing dandelion
seeds into a swirling crystal ball,

broken wall. Armageddon roof.
Love letters changed hands while you
lived at home, in Lithuania, with seven
siblings. A twenty-year old married

woman waited for her husband—my father-
to-be. It must have angered you living
those years apart before and after my birth.
Together, they escaped their homeland,

fearing Russian Communists. Secrets
disclosed Das Reichland sent you, born
in Philadelphia, to Duderstadt, a German
slave labor munitions, work-camp.

Father was crated to St. Andreasberg,
a silver mining town now a ski resort,
doctoring hunched backs carrying quartz-calcite,
lead, copper, arsenic, and ore in lower Saxony.

Agamemnon dead.
Your rose-gold diamond ring rests in a drawer
smaller than years remember.

peace
stands at the crossing
beyond love and hate

Moira Shearer, *The Red Shoes*

On the first page of my dreambook
the ballerina's scarlet, satin-layered
tutu twirled across the cinema screen.
Bouquets cover satin toe shoes like Moira
Shearer in the *The Red Shoes* movie.

She ponders between marriage or ballet
as pirouettes twirled through the darkness
then leaped in front of a roaring train.
Only her flaming shoes remained.

Years pass, my pointe shoes and lambswool
toe pads rest on the laundry room shelf
begging to dance, but soon to be incinerated.

Prana Life Force, Universal Sea of Energy

About 60 million prisoners perished in Stalin's gulag.

Father, did you sterilize broken bodies
bundled higher than the Elbrus mountains?
England, Russia, and the US agreed under the
Yalta Conference to trade you like cattle
for free labor to Stalingrad's gulag.

Did you sanitize the Volga River's stench?
Odors linger still. Released without a reason
over seventy-years ago, were you considered
German, or Lithuanian by birth?
Answers tailgate the wind gods.

Silent years multiply under a withering sun.
I touch these stale, fading papers again and again.
Your prints remain—remind that on ten occasions
machine guns targeted your head and heart.
Two questions fired: Name? Occupation?

Silence streaked across charcoal skies.
Questions multiply, nestle inside MG 42s.
Somehow you survived. I repeat your name,
your life. Define immigrant, define DP,
define love.

"Prana" in Sanskrit means life force, energy and vital principle to manifest energy in the universe. Father's Lithuanian name is Pranas.

Anatomy of a Heart, the Aorta of Mine

There are no gulls screaming in this graveyard
far from the Baltic Sea. My poems cannot excavate
nations, nor people like Milosz. *Schatze*,

sweetheart, rips open a shrapnel heart
under Father's century-old tomb.

Ghosts whisper, words line the Ohio River.
Look not into my eyes or between lines.
I cannot comprehend Father's thoughts

whether to silence their presence or welcome
them home. If you prop open the front door

with your boot, I will slam it shut—pour millet
on your tombstone with the beak of a pigeon,
eyes of a hawk torching: photos, paintings, pottery,

birth, marriage certificates, and bank accounts.
A parakeet lies buried in the backyard

under shaggy bark. Auricle, ventricle, mistral,
vena cava, listen to me—a German shepherd
claws at my front door. Father leans

into the gravestone, his name engraves
the last line. Dearest, Schatze.

He Is Ready

A grave—
His coffin
Suspends
On Father's tongue
In Mother's country
A 400-year-old tombstone
Waits

Guilty, but guiltless
Prisoner of wars
A fishhook hung
Between eyes
But he survived
Frozen tundra
Without a jacket, boots
Or warm kisses

Barefoot
He drove
Into the journey
Searching for home
And a place to cry

Marymount Hospital, Cleveland

Father never on labored a farm as did his parents,
their parents, and great grandparents. Slender fingers
never touched piano keys or squeezed

a grandchild with nighttime prayers filled
with storybook kisses. Skilled fingers stitched skins,
slipping through lives untouched, yet touched.

Lou Gehrig's Disease claimed each muscle in atrophy.
Hospital walls bore witness as my five-year-old daughter,
Marielle, sat in a chair across the room, then lifted her violin

from the case. Standing erect, nimble fingers cavorted
concerto strings. White sheets covered Father's skeletal body
stretched captive under Vivaldi's spell. His muscles

involuntarily convulsed an avalanche from head to toe.
A thunderous applause under shivering snow. I swab Father's
throat for an extra breath. Some bed boils never heal.

Your left hand points to orange juice.

DAZED MEMORIAL, BURNT FLESH LINGERS

Walking to the river—Father's funeral wakens this sleep
deprived heart, a man who survived Nazi concentration
camps and the Gulag, he served others.
    Sister called: *Come tomorrow to the Bedford*
    Funeral Home at 1 pm. Father is dead.

My children stayed home. I clutched a borrowed Bible
in my right hand quoting marked passages from Isaiah 43:2
to four people. The priest's eyes glued mine, shocked
    in disbelief as if I stole his verses and sermon.
    His erratic, memorial phrases stumbled

across the walls. Mother's tears hunched over Father's body:
A doctor in a cardboard box! I thought, *Who put him there?*
Then she commanded, *Follow me.* I obeyed like a child
    without question, stepping down steep, short,
    cold concrete steps. Sister leaned on her husband's

shoulder, a banister supported my confused, frail body
as if stuffed in a garbage bag marching to a forsaken Gulag.
A body slid through a metal door, the latch clicked
    separating our bodies forever. Clenching
    the Bible, someone flipped a switch—

flames roared through the peephole, enveloping every spirit.
The ground shook our bones. Mother said, *We must be sure*
these are his ashes. Smoke-filtered skies inflamed breath.

    The odor of burnt flesh penetrates our skin.
    Later, I kicked off my shoes standing in a shallow,
    cool brook gazing into cumulus clouds.

Because My Hands Have Always Known...

I cannot hold yours, Father, long cremated.
Mother said, *Follow me below earth's steps.*

I obeyed. The switch flipped father's
body Mad Red. Was I wearing Rothko's

black or Klimt's gold kimono?
Earlier in a trance, I held a borrowed Bible

firm against my body quoting passages.
The minister heckled. Limping into the Mad Red car,

I drove to the Cape looking for a seahorse
to carry me home. Because my hands have always

known labor—what do they know now?
Arthritic wrists, hips, and ankles hobble

inflamed Madder Red. I want to be 60 again,
melt amber within my breath. Remember 20?

The Tree of Life

In dreams, Father's body trembles,
        each vibration stirs my gut
Forget Georgia O'Keeffe's flower-love.
        This is ALS.

Listen to missiles soar above barrier reefs
        throwing mothers and children into an abyss.
Look past concentration camps and a handful of survivors
        beyond annihilated familial remains.

Depleted love hovers over Sudan, Yemen, Syria, Kashmir,
        Rwanda, Ukraine. Do not forget Stalin's forced famine.
Six-million Ukrainians exterminated and three million
        children churned into compost.

Does history repeat? Grief multiplies. Repeat
        after me: *l'amour, je t'aime, liebe, amare, myliu.*
Wrap these words around your wounds,
        and bowels. Let them fly clinging to earth.

Watch words spin, gripping you and me
        in Red Canna, Black Iris love.

Lifeline Epigraph

Frangible skin maps wisdom
        and prison camps that have borne
more than one lifeline. Cities change
        names removing atrocities from globes,
maps, and history. Stalingrad is now Volgograd.
        Father's photo props against the piano's
leg, proof he survived WWII walking this earth.
        My back turns fearful of disapproving eyes,
then knife the Hippocratic Oath from a matt
        that hung in his office. Scripted
Old English reminders sworn to Aesculapius,
        Apollo, Pythagoras, and all the Baltic gods.
Spores escape into air. I swear you did no harm burning
        the moldy Hippocratic Oath without despair.

Benediction at Bad Sassendorf Farm

An overheard conversation about Tamara, 1945

Parachute bombs drop bodies one-by-one,
frozen in time. Giants pull triggers as stars
burst into bombs on Shakespeare's stage.

Tamara runs to the outhouse near river's basin, gunned
by plane or roaming tank, shot in her tracks
by a Brit, American, or Canadian.

Witness blood ooze and curl alizarin pathways,
the stench thickens stale air calling an army of ants
to rescue. Shards of war-torn flesh

sanctify afterlife while crimson ribbons and medals
turn into ceremonial honors. Skull fragments
seal mortal secrets. Who can provide

a proper burial for this sister, cousin, aunt,
or mother never-to be? Toss a dark lady
rose to the wind gods,

watch petals cling branch to twig.
Throw a bloodstone into the river
of absolution. Sign a cross. A cross.

an orchid emerges
under the light
Venus

The Moon at 3 A.M.

Look I have dreamed another dream. And this time he sun,
the moon, and the eleven stars bowed down to me.
—Genesis 37:9

Tonight, Mėnulis, moon is 30% brighter
than the last 15 years, 13% larger than in 2008.
It swallows the sky.

The schoolhouse teacher with candy wrapper lips
stands on a back porch facing the Buck Moon's
eyelash glow. Diamond

studs blaze the skies more radiant than Vakarinė,
evening star. Venus, sweetens the roundness
of your face against July's soft shoulder.

Leaves shudder and bow to Mėnulis, our moon goddess.
Tonight, let us toast myth with wine, a song,
and dance. Accept the unknowns.

Dancing with Dvorak

Severance Hall Concert

Relax, breathe deep, rotate your head,
shoulders and back like a swan.
Exhale on the downbeat. Inhale soft
notes that flit from your neck to mine,
an instrumental synopsis from Strad
to pen. Music swirls inside walls,
appeasing the gods.

A twitch of an eye or hand dissolves.
Heads nod in a breeze of gratitude.
Tonight is clear, several stars
swell through the ceiling.
Aušrinė, Vakarinė, and Indraja.

Gut strings straddle violin moons.
Seal this concert with parted lips.
Another movement twirls rapid high.
Swift feet quicken, toes arabesque,
shooting arrows part the sky.
Cervical bones rotate in slow motion.

Rigid muscles relax into smoothness.
Don't forget the back. Women
hold the weight of the world
between shoulder blades on axis
between wars spoken, then buried.

Dvorak, my favorite word for blue skies is music.

Lonesome Lock, Peninsula Towpath

The winds bluster and howl up to 60 mph.
  My husband says, *Let's take a hike,*
listen to the Cuyahoga rapids pulse. My heart rushes
  with the river as if we are one.
Our paths illuminate before darkness
  consumes and the full moon
stretches over ancient trees. I skip
  over torn tree limbs. Several
gray-haired bikers ride against Superstorm
  Sandy on our three-mile hike.
Voices echo. Savage gusts slash hat,
  jacket, gloves, even sox. A lone
squirrel crosses our path uncovering moon's
  white shadow. Somewhere between
  heaven and the blue heron I stand.

STARDUST

We are built of star stuff
—Carl Sagan, *Cosmos*

Perhaps we were a figment in the black hole
energizing explosions? Perhaps earth envelops
seabirds, man, and dust particles in the universe
before combustion, before stars negate
themselves and planets follow?

Take a moment observe the light
and dust particles multiplying in my home.

Examine early sex remains
in newly discovered Myanmar amber.
Pollen tubes penetrate a well preserved
flower's stigma.

For now I am safe among the trees,
tender roots carry fine years.
Let me disappear inside the spinning
galaxy of raw Lithuanian amber
proving bees have derived from wasps.

Perhaps we carry the same signature,
the same atoms as Venus, Mars, Saturn,
all the planets and stars. Perhaps the black hole
will never disappear or lose energy? It is impossible
The black hole will never decrease over time,
Stephen Hawking's theory is confirmed.

A galaxy spins out-of-control as I flush toilets,
vacuum kitty litter and migrant dust-balls.
Mundane tasks require universal order.

What Shall We Remember of this Earth?

when coyotes and wolves are poisoned
        and Nagasaki ghosts invade our minds?
Will we recall nuclear disasters and forsaken
        concentration camps of buried battered bones
fertilizing mother earth? Who will revive

the Black Hole and glaciers for spirit bears
        to guide and teach the young to hunch their bodies,
arms hovering overhead under desks,
        in fear of death? In grade school,
I crunched under daily desk drills

waiting for blasting bombs in Hildesheim,
        I walked on asphalt analyzing new buildings
and streets against cobblestones across the street,
        such a visible divide. Today, Corona hovers
the globe as books disappear from libraries and desks.

Scorched trees fill millions of acres. Does anyone
        cringe at our antibiotic food supply while genetically
modified DNA's multiply in our bodies? Even
        the Chesapeake Bay carries farm feces into rivers.
Worn shoes line a river of stones. Arms embrace
        the thousand-year *Stelmužė* Oak with Amazing Grace.

dry leaves curl
from heaven's fall
a painter's brush

VOICES FROM THE RHONE

When I was twenty-one, Father said to me:
Meet me at river's edge, we'll jet to Arles.
          Surely this is your dream, my child.

This good doctor will stitch your ear
so you will always hear me right.
          Do not worry about medical bills,

I will check all statements twice.
Your second-floor room will overlook
          Van Gogh's courtyard.

What an honor to watch the squirrels
and blue jays fetch seeds, darling.
          Brighten your senses,

pluck fresh Provence lavender, inhale
with closed eyes. Tourists unfold the season
          in early May

when plastered walls glisten with fresh paint.
Beware of fierce mistral *Provençal* winds
          blowing candles into smoke.

Steep stairs may be your downfall. Remain
in your room. But, showers are down the hall.
          I'll supply all necessary *papier de toilette.*

Guests are forbidden, love. In one year
you'll hear me right, we'll toast to Camille
          and Vincent in the courtyard.

Paint to your heart's content. I'll sell your paintings
or light a giant pit honoring the gods in splendor and delight.
          But, you must marry whom I choose.

Die Künstlerroman

An artist's novel

Bleeding fingernails squeeze dry sunflower seeds into the Rhone. Our heroine steeps green tea, vodka sweetened with a touch of lavender. See the empty cups lining riverbeds?

Nightfall rests inside the plaza embracing cosmic spears across the dark universe. Our heroine waits to be found. Frolicking ghosts pass *L'Espace,* that moss filled fountain in Van Gogh's Arles, and gulp green absinthe in asylum.

Stalking riverbeds, painting crimson lanterns searching for a poppy-red dress. Bare toes rake the Rhone. Her worn shoes drift into the orb of night, red-suede, size 10.

Take Me Home, Vincent

> *The Large Plane Trees* (Road Menders at Saint Rémy) 1889, by Vincent Van Gogh, The Cleveland Museum of Art

Under the sirocco—

Walking from asylum
your footprints never fade.
The worn leather of death
passes plane trees lining streets
a year before your death. I observe
your oil painting, the feverish, thick
impasto brush sprints across a red,
checkerboard tablecloth under a make-believe
canvas. Street workers forever frozen—
your calloused hands once brushed rats
off this painting. I stare at your palette:
zinc yellow, van dyke brown, madder red,
vermillion, cobalt blue, French ultramarine,
cadmium yellow, viridian, and emerald
green under zinc white clouds, just as it was.
Your paintings forever smile at death.

TRAVELING INCOGNITO

Faith, a Baptist tradition, water in a tub blown
and fused into a new life. Memories live across
the Hope Ocean, miracles stain my teeth crimson.

August. That Monday, a wind-driven Parisian night,
I stood on a bench at Shakespeare & Co. Bookstore.
Jonathan's voice sank into my bones announcing:
This evening we are most fortunate to have a famous American
actress. Unfortunately, I cannot divulge her name, she travels
incognito. I squint, searching for that face then read
my poems before the Notre Dame.

September. Before the jazz band rocked "Cafe Noir,"
Fauzi asked, *Are you a famous actress from The States—*
your name escapes. Who are you? My smile jets from Ohio.
Do my hands and my voice belong to someone else
traveling in disguise like Mia Farrow without make-
up sporting a short, new haircut?

October. I wait under a blazing sun, half-a-star
while he twirled my hand across the room.
We danced slow moves. I never had enough.

November. Scanning World War letters and photos:
the landlady stole baby's milk. Blank copper
eyes clung to my Mother's empty breasts.
Women stopped pointed at the pram outside
Notre Dame and baby's shaved head.
Parisians called Mother crazy.

Parisienne Feet

Metro map in hand, passing street signs,
nibbling petit fours, in six weeks I shed
ten pounds walking, finally discover Musée Picasso
in the Marais district. Guernica spears guts

unfolding war trials and tribulations. I touch
this monochromatic painting, a knife-tongue bull
strikes the canvas. Black and white oil pigments dismember
a human-horse. I miss galleria's air and daggers
striking after dark. Picasso, permit me to remain,
inhale your paintings after dark. I promise to behave.

An American woman celebrates her last afternoon in Paris.
Where should she be, but under the linden tree vowing
to return to Musée Rodin. Are promises made to be broken,
released, or forgotten? I cannot forget Camille Claudel,
Auguste Rodin, or baguettes? The garden fountain sprays
across stolen sculptural moments.

In prison, Ugalino lurched hesitant over his son's starved body,
debating whether to lunge into his famished flesh.
Both starved. Then I boldly add Camille Claudel's name
to the Musée Rodin sign, compelled to blaze Madame
Beuret's portrait, who tried to knife Camille at a brasserie.
Triangular love.

I sip café crème in the garden, stirring my porcelain cup
with a golden demi-spoon. Drooling. In this chair,
I release years of craving.

Let Me Die in Paris

—after Cesar Vallejo

Listen to the French roll tongues at Cafe Bastille,
watching spring bouquets stroll far and near,
so many luscious bites from which to choose—
Decisions at Le Pompidou, outdoor dejeuner in the nude

with Manet, resurrecting portals of Notre Dame
with a palette of petite-four and brie. Perhaps,
I shall die exiled to the second-floor library
at Shakespeare and Company Bookstore, a stone's throw

from la Seine. Or, rest upon Napoleon's short, royal
bed stuffed in a corner of Musée du Louvre?
Surely I shall give up the flame holding a baccarat
of Moët & Chandon under Auguste Rodin's watchful

eye as Camille Claudel dances our way. Rose Beuret,
hangs on the wall glaring at our footsteps. Never mind
sweet espresso, pain aux chocolat, or baquettes trailing
a sparrow's path. Perhaps I shall shred millions

of letters from Picasso Musée, replace each with a poem?
It will be early June before the flocks arrive, the sun
will shine and Mediterranean stars will sift through
our fingers as we dance under a sultry moon.

Just let me be.

Dungeons and Catacombs

Dark mold does not fumigate
earth. Cordwood eyes roll
into my own bagged bones.

I caress buried skeletons
beneath Notre Dame catacombs
sifting ashes of those once loved,

forgiving self for this birth. Fixed
in eternity, I reach for your hand,
touch the moon with the tip of my bow

connecting heaven to earth. Wishes
bloom on portraits and graves.
I tape charcoal drawings to walls
blowing thistles into dusty swirls.

Outdoors, breathing fresh air,
fluttering wings wave good-bye
to the keeper of hours. I throw

a trail of breadcrumbs among blackbirds
and muted swans. The sun slits open
my fragile chest as umber leaves rest.

I walk along moonlit path reading
a letter, light warming back.
Mama is dead.

Because My Heart Has Always Known...

Love is not a birthright
but a privilege
searching
through thorns
for my cocker spaniel
shredded
by a passing car.

His urine forever
streamed down Lowe Street.
Years seek forgiveness
for the rope-leash noose
around his neck, Mother
could not afford a leader.

Scrub resin-stained tears
off the mirror for Mona
Lisa's disguised smile
igniting hidden paths.
Guilt rages inside
ultramarine skies.

Darling

Why am I alone, Mother asked?
        Shallow roots bury thoughts.
At the edge of night, your back turned

at the studio. Later, I offered
        your ashes to *Vēja Māte,*
Mother of the Wind.

To my dead aunts and cousin--
        Why was I never told?
Shivering maples seek answers.

Several oaks root our secrets.
        Frost comes, everything's undone,
bodies sway in the wind.

Mother Rose—Why
        did you leave me home alone,
frigid under the table

inside the locked steamer trunk?
        I searched for breath.
An angel plays the flute

while the harp saves all.
        Crimson roses crown Mary's head.
Smiles rejoice, it's Christmas day

in the morn. Adult laughter
        echoed through the apartment.
My coal filled stocking overflowed,

stacked higher than Cousin Bill's,
        next to our coal furnace.
My tears flooded the living room.

Below the Super Blood Moon

A tank
roams
searching
for answers
in a desert,
I water
old roots

November's
orchid blooms
against window
stark snows
as humble
buds burst
below the
Super Blood
Moon

Sun's
shadow
lights a path
to a new
birth

Reminders

Tonight, I read dusted birthday and holiday wishes:
Daughter, you left home too early. How dare you marry?

Did mother ever embrace love? She remembered
and repeated murmurs under breath.

Shrinking bones read forsaken letters
nestled in brown cardboard boxes with salvaged

stamps from Germany, Austria, Russia,
and the U.S. which once cost three cents.

My muscles never forget blasting bombs in Germany.
The birds, squirrels, dogs, and I convulse

during July Fourth sky reminders
that bombs reign forever. A rocket blasts

out-of-bounds. A car exhaust fan
swirls in darkness. finding another scribble,

*Maybe it is good to write…*Mother's hand-written
letters invite frolicking ghosts.

Forgive Me

I am the bad child, the greedy child
who does not fit into the scheme
of things. I do not deserve
Mother's ancestral amber.

This child only thinks of herself
wrapped in an unblemished
polar-white, hooded bunny coat
with button-tail eyes

crunched next to the coal furnace.
Mother Rose rips the coat off my back
and gifts it to a worthy child—the French teacher's
daughter. Was the rabbit skin strung

to a leather strap for protection, decoration,
or luck? Listen to the tears
of the hungry, primordial child.
No one sees her bleeding body ooze

a trail of Baltic pinesap across virgin snows.
Years pass, Mother asks, *Why am I forgotten?*
I want to slap her face so she will recognize her firstborn
as the first pinesap oozed a river

from her thighs, 60 million years ago.
Warrior Mother extends her final breath
for two years on a hospital bed. Hearing faded,
limbs stiff oak branches too heavy to turn

or learn these words, *Love you child.*
From the pillow she asks,
Where are my children? Why am I forgotten?
The slammed door echoes down the hall.

I sit on stones
listen to ohms
drift past

GRANT WOOD WOULD NEVER MIND

Oil painting *American Gothic*, 1930, Art Institute of Chicago.

Suitcases in the basement, filled with black and white photos rest through nights without given names, no clues as to who's who. An Inheritance of sorts? What would you do, garage sale the whole family? This isn't really my family, you know. My husband doesn't know what to do with his relatives' either—make-up names, stories, habits, or games for the kids?

These photos were taken in Latvia, next door to Lithuania. Many comment Lithuania, who? A disease? Baltics, where? Balkan, no. See the stern faces—I could honor each with a pitchfork or hang them in an ethnic museum. Grant Wood wouldn't mind turning *American Gothic* into Latvian Gothic. The past is relevant.

I'll title these photos. Title yours. Give someone a break—incinerate past names, trash, and recycle. Do not whisper—how could she? Relish the present, the names of poets at the writer's table. Enjoy coffee and sticky buns. Get your fingers dirty, smell the cinnamon, check out each draft horse across the street. Leave your name at the front door.

Morning Wind Whispers

Dedicated to the poet, Major Ragain

In a deserted mineshaft, blackness
throbs against autumn leaves.
Sunlight writes on mountain flames,
Maj's arctic breath seals a kiss
on my sleepless forehead.

The hallway vibrates, dissonant steps
silence distant moons. I wake to write
your words before the kiss dissipates.
Premature swollen grief, satin tears
fade on soft, pink rose petals.

A Tsunami Dream

A tidal wave approaches, threatening
clouds search for one person.
        I escape the late rawness,
        zip amber rings into a satin pouch
        and run into panic-dazed faces

herded into Nazi railroad cars zooming away.
Witness the sea gather strength
        from swirling gray forces. Hydraulic
        waters rise high on land,
        deserted farms, and cars.

I stand, continue the flight.
No place to hide or retreat, many die.
        On Lake Erie I reach toward nimbus
        clouds, tailwinds call my name.
        We both live, my love.

Along the Curonian Spit

Find warmth between
the pines of two countries
past the forgotten
wooden rake
and shattered granite
sundial, stretching
light into darkness
along the spit, *Raganų Kalnas*—
Witches Hill fills shadows
with devil's oak, hand-carved
for each hour through many years.

Children slide down tongues
stepping on the stairs of her teeth
exhausted, under gateway warnings:

> *Dance, but do not*
> *step on my shoes*
> *or look for my feet.*
> *How I miss my toes.*
> *It's midnight*
> *my carriage waits*
> *and the rooster moans.*

Explore the ancient
Baltic shores, curl toes
into white sand sifting
precious nuggets
through fingertips
like a child kissing stones.
Grab an amber nugget
hold it tight—claim life
before the birds of dawn
wake, searching for the soul
of a tiger that purrs.

Fire Shadows

After *The Persistence of Memory* by Salvador Dalí, 1931

Stopwatches of the universe

drape bones

skulls of departed dreams.

Fire shadows skip across your face

into cerulean skies. The pocket watch

gains momentum. A closed eye

centipede collects wounds.

Thor Carries Many Names

The great winds sway, leaves shudder
          bow in silence. Howling breaks the lull.
A lone sparrow chants in treble keys,
          a crow closes the distant storm
between us. Jets soar through heaven's stillness.
          Thunder-clap, a welcome thief feeds
the landscape, quenching summer's desiccation.

Listen! The slap stings into one continuous
          chord like streamers racing from the sky.
Thor, the thunder god carries many names;
          Zeus, Jupiter, Perkūnas. He pounces
then roars while Mėnulis, the moon goddess
          sleeps with Saulė, our sun, they fidget
between Thor's piercing applause. A distant train
          hums, emeralds burst. Listen to Thor,
his pangs roar, circle, and sweep as the wind chimes
          Om Mani Padme Hum.

Note to a Fledgling

I dialed my childhood
and no one answered.

Is your mother mine as well?
Chantilly's backyard grave

sinks deeper as church
bells echo across Mill Pond.

Never trust a starling.
I carry two in my pocket.

Massage the Surface of Pain

Remember youthful love when a hug
raced warmth throughout your body
and daybreak blazed windows of hopeful
miracles? I dreamed of a grandmother
caressing all my shameful doubts. Once,
in Lithuania, she walked to the market,
but never returned home.

Captured or killed by Russian Communists,
she disappeared from our landscape.
Never found. Light flings through
my Cape Cod dreams of ocean roses,
star flowers, and water lilies. I lie
between blades of sea grass.

Footprints In Snow

Snowflake stars sparkle on the window. A moment captures
fragile evergreen branches in the essence of sticking together.
No two flakes are alike, formations entice like crystal books
waiting in the basement for lantern's glow.

Fresh snow records paw tracks circling the house. Squirrel
nails etch the driveway. Mama Fox returns checking my backyard
compost. Several kits romp and play, smiles bloom on frigid
faces. A doe and her proud buck stroll through the park.

They stop and check. Years ago, the city permitted bow
and arrow hunting, erasing deer footprints, but never forgotten.
Hiking Sunny Lake a slim figure skates gracefully, holding a five-
year old daughter. Their private, rectangular arena is clean.

Glee follows each balletic glide. Snow and sunshine embrace
diamond trees during January skies. A neighbor's icicles hang
from roof lines. Across the street, grandkids slide down
the slope, giggling in frosty air.

peppermint tea
I cup the unknown
silence

Through Trees

I face the rising Blue Moon as the globe
of night unlocks a trunkful of wishes and hope.

Ancestors planted trees under the buck-
thunder moon for sweet bounty. Medeine,

Lady of Trees, goddess of woods and hare
grants peace to roadside plantings,

crossings, holidays, and other holy places.
Birth, a wedding tree; when a child is born

plant another. If a beloved dies, root an oak.
Plant seed-bearing junipers, wormwood,

or silverweed roses to shade the dead.
I pray through trees of thanks that I may

not fell a single one without holy need,
nor step on a blooming field.

May I always plant trees, sit on rooftops,
and walk below the crescent moon.

Gintaras, Baltic Amber

Bee trapped, buried under pine
sap resin, the mermaid Jūratė, lifts
three-dimensional animal spirits
into transparent legends. Her fingers

gloss fossil remains releasing
a lifetime of beetles, spiders,
and wasps. Expose and release
your own prehistoric creatures.

Wipe, dust, polish embedded fossil
remains—release a lifetime of beetles,
spiders, and wasps. Expose your own
prehistoric creatures.

Hang precious nuggets from closet
rods, toss them into a roaring fire,
collect ancient benedictions, sleep
carefully with a tarnished talisman.

Catch breath on pure linen for Jūratė
will toss burnished amber, silver, and gold
from her ring finger to yours. Count
to ten, inhale the Baltic blessings.
Release, relax.

A Wedding Song for My Daughter, Lara and Daniel

The soul: a widening sky with thousands of candles
—Rumi

Love is a tree whose branches
reach into eternity, firm roots
set deep within earth. Spring hums,
birds flit in the rose garden. Listen
to the music whisper, winter's ended.
Daffodils and sage cannot control
their laughter—the nightingale returns
to sing as master of all birds.

The feast is set, the wind pours wine.
We gather to celebrate the union of love,
bonds transform hardship into luck.
This wedding is a braiding joining
two into one as the sun melts a lake of ice.
Untangle old knots someone else tied
for you. Tie this new one together, today.
Prepare, enter this marriage as if crossing
the Alps and going home.

Pledge truth. Find a failing,
a sweet door opens to a garden.
Make a bonfire, be warmed, burn
old and newfound stupidities.
Padlock your initials to a bridge,
toss the key into rapid rivers.
Push back darkness, sing honey
and salt to the source of bread, life,
and the play of rainbows. Braid spring
blossoms throughout summer and fall.

Plant your orchard, prepare winter's harvest,
delight with years of prosperity. Let us dance
under the galaxy of Venus and Mars toasting
Krug Grande Cuvée champagne under the stars.

Lithuanian Style Cold Beets Soup, *Šaltibarščiai*

Summer's grocery list: hard-boiled eggs,
whole red beets, potatoes, cucumbers, chives
or green onions, and a bouquet of garden-fresh dill.

Scrub beets, boil for 20 minutes. Drain, cool,
scrape skins; slice and boil in your largest pot.
Fear not, if hands turn scarlet, this ritual

brightens visions. Run cold water over
boiled eggs with a swift hand, rolling motion.
Peel the shells, chop, set aside. Spend an afternoon

with a razor knife. If blood-stained fingers
drip into soup, that's fine. Blood and beets
go hand-to-hand. Dice remaining ingredients.

Fingers are created to touch and feel pain.
Now sit, rest, and stir this pot with a hand-
carved wooden spoon like the one Father

used to whack my derrière with. Sprinkle
salt and pepper into the tear laden pot.
Cool, scoop soup into bowls, add sour cream

for the brightest pink. Stir, inhale, waken
all senses. Boil, peel, diced potatoes in another
pot. Drain, set on a platter beside bowls of soup

topped with fresh, diced dill. Cool. Sit, exhale
the chore is done. Feast, salute summer
for all ancestors sit at this table.

Acknowledgements

I bow in gratitude to Larry Smith, Barbara Sabol, John Guzowski, Pam Uschuk, Algis Ruksenas, Conor Bracken, in memoriam Alynn Mahle, The Ohio Haiku Association and all my cherished friends for spurring me onward with this heartfelt manuscript.

Grateful acknowledgements to the editors and staff of the following publications in which these poems have been published: *Ascent Aspirations, Blue Nib, Cleveland Scene, Common Threads Magazine, First Literary Review, Fourth & Sycamore, Gingerbread House Literary Magazine, Golden Haiku, Hessler Street Anthology, Liberty House Journal Anthology, Lone Star Review, Poetry Barn, Poetry Distillery, Qarrtsiluni, Rat's Ass Review, Seashores Haiku, Sheila Na Gig, The Lake Poetry, The Raven Review, The Wanderer Brush, the Art of Haiga* by Ion Codrescu, *Touch: A Journal of Healing, Whispers Magazine.*

Notes

The list of Lithuanian gods is based upon scarce written sources, folklore, and myth. Aušrinė is the feminine deity of the Morning Star; Venus, is the daughter of Dievas, God, she burns morning fires for her mother, Saulė, the Sun. Vakarinė, Evening Star also prepares the bed for Saulė, the fertility goddess of life, warmth, and health. Indraja is also known as Jupiter.

"Earth Mother, Žemyna": Goddess Žemyna concerns multiplication and fertility, she creates life out of herself performing the miracle of renewal. The act accords with an old European belief that seasonal wakening, growing, fattening, and dying were interdependent among humans, animals, and plants (Marija Gubaitis). During the late 17th century a Lithuanian priestess presided in a black suckling pig offering during the harvest festival, as to the Grecian Demeter.

Perkunas: Lithuanian God of thunder and lightning resembles Zeus and Jupiter. Even though Christian missionaries cut down the sacred oak forests, perpetual oak fires continued to blaze. Black heifer, goat, or cock sacrifices were offered to Perkunas during droughts to save their crops. Many gathered to feast carrying a bowl of beer twice around the fire then poured the beer into flames while praying. (Sir James George Frazer)

Ars Moriendi: "The Art of Dying", a 15th century manual. Terra signifies the Roman Earth Goddess.

"Anatomy of a Heart, the Aorta of Mine": Schatze; German term of endearment.

"Among Your Effects, a Photograph": Mamytė Lithuanian term of endearment, mother.

"Eye of a Tiger": According to the Eastern culture when a tiger dies its soul-spirit penetrates earth and turns to amber. *Amber: Golden Gem of the Ages* by Patty C. Rice.

"Thor Carries Many Names": In Tibetan Buddhism, the mantra *Om Mani Padme Hum* signifies the impure as well as exalted body, speech and mind; the jewel lotus.

About the Author

As a child, most Saturdays were filled with inspirational drawing and painting classes at the Chicago Art Institute, this instilled a life-long affair with the arts.

A former KSU art professor once remarked my sketchbooks looked like poetry. Who would have guessed this observation predicted a weaving of art and poems?

For years, I have combined my art and poems by creating artist books. Intuitively, my art flows in a constant flux of discovery that employs both sides of the brain. Detail and action influence my creative process by color or the absence of color. Often my paintings reflect fantasy based upon memory and experience. Layers of paint may reveal abstractions that expand the canvas. At other times my art begins in reality whether a human form or a still life arrangement.

My professional practice nurtures and propels towards continual experimentation with limitless supplies, as well as the action of brush springing against canvas. Solutions to one puzzle emerge while in gentle contemplation. You are invited into my world of possibilities! A painting can be a lyrical poem that merges art and psycho-biography into unique flowing lines and amorphous organic forms to evoke raw emotions.

I participated in international book exhibitions and enjoyed a retrospective at the Moos Gallery in Hudson, Artists Archive in

Cleveland, The Cleveland Art Museum, Bind-O-Rama's 20th Anniversary, also a Provincetown Fellowship and Residency at the Fine Arts Work Center, as well as winner of the Akron Art Museum's New Words Competition, etc. It was a privileged to read my poems twice at The Shakespeare & Company Bookstore, in Paris, In *Baltic Amber in a Chest,* I share my Baltic heritage including myths coupled with modern historic writing in various poetic forms mingling personal experiences within narrative mythic pastorals revealing powerful World War II events nestled in my genes.

Perhaps these shared stories will reflect your family's history as we are all inter-connected in some way. I am compelled to share these personal observations which may bring clarity and closure while opening new doors for fresh air. Tears shed because our experiences relate to millions of families on this planet.

Books by Bottom Dog Press

Harmony Series

Baltic Amber in a Chest: Poems, by Clarissa Jakobsons, 104 pgs., $16
The Pears: Poems, by Larry Smith, 66 pgs, $15
Without a Plea, by Jeff Gundy, 96 pgs, $16
Taking a Walk in My Animal Hat, by Charlene Fix, 90 pgs, $16
Earnest Occupations, by Richard Hague, 200 pgs, $18
Pieces: A Composite Novel, by Mary Ann McGuigan, 250 pgs, $18
Crows in the Jukebox: Poems, by Mike James, 106 pgs, $16
Portrait of the Artist as a Bingo Worker: A Memoir, by Lori Jakiela, 216 pgs, $18
The Thick of Thin: A Memoir, by Larry Smith, 238 pgs, $18
Cold Air Return: A Novel, by Patrick Lawrence O'Keeffe, 390 pgs, $20
Flesh and Stones: A Memoir, by Jan Shoemaker, 176 pgs, $18
Waiting to Begin: A Memoir, by Patricia O'Donnell, 166 pgs, $18
And Waking: Poems, by Kevin Casey, 80 pgs, $16
Both Shoes Off: Poems, by Jeanne Bryner, 112 pgs, $16
Abandoned Homeland: Poems, by Jeff Gundy, 96 pgs, $16
Stolen Child: A Novel, by Suzanne Kelly, 338 pgs, $18
The Canary: A Novel, by Michael Loyd Gray, 196 pgs, $18
On the Flyleaf: Poems, by Herbert Woodward Martin, 106 pgs, $16
The Harmonist at Nightfall: Poems of Indiana, by Shari Wagner, 114 pgs, $16
Painting Bridges: A Novel, by Patricia Averbach, 234 pgs, $18
Ariadne & Other Poems, by Ingrid Swanberg, 120 pgs, $16
The Search for the Reason Why: New and Selected Poems, by Tom Kryss, 192 pgs, $16
Kenneth Patchen: Rebel Poet in America, by Larry Smith,
Revised 2nd Edition, 326 pgs, Cloth $28
Selected Correspondence of Kenneth Patchen,
Edited with introduction by Allen Frost, Paper $18/ Cloth $28
Awash with Roses: Collected Love Poems of Kenneth Patchen,
Eds. Laura Smith and Larry Smith
with introduction by Larry Smith, 200 pgs, $16
Breathing the West: Great Basin Poems, by Liane Ellison Norman, 96 pgs, $16
Maggot: A Novel, by Robert Flanagan, 262 pgs, $18
American Poet: A Novel, by Jeff Vande Zande, 200 pgs, $18
The Way-Back Room: Memoir of a Detroit Childhood, by Mary Minock, 216 pgs, $18

Bottom Dog Press, Inc.
P.O. Box 425 /Huron, Ohio 44839
http://smithdocs.net

CPSIA information can be obtained
at www.ICGtesting.com
Printed in the USA
BVHW032124210123
656729BV00027B/1087

9 781947 504370